THE STONE

THE STONE
NEW & SELECTED POEMS FROM ASIA

by
Joe Survant

Accents Publishing • Lexington, Kentucky • 2026

Printed in the United States of America

Accents Publishing
Editor: Katerina Stoykova
Cover Photo: Joe Survant

Library of Congress Control Number: 2026931378
ISBN: 978-1-961127-22-7
First Edition

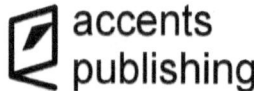

Accents Publishing is an independent press for brilliant voices. For a catalog of current and upcoming titles, please visit us on the Web at

www.accents-publishing.com

CONTENTS

For Teoh Boon Seong
(1947–2008)

who showed me the way

The ocean pours
through a jar, and you might say it

swims 'inside' the fish! This mystery gives peace to your
longing and makes the road home home.

—*The Soul of Rumi*, Coleman Barks

FOREWORD

Many of these poems were written while teaching in the mid 80s at the Universiti Sains Malaysia in Penang, Malaysia. Some of them were later published in Singapore in 2001 as *The Presence of Snow in the Tropics*. Others are from travels in SE Asia over the past 30 years. Even though it has been eight years since I was last in that part of the world, poems still continue to appear as if they were dormant chrysalises waiting for a signal to change and emerge. Once, on a weekend camping trip with three of my Malay students in the jungle of East Malaysia, I was awakened by some noise in the undergrowth. While my students slept soundly, I searched the dense forest with my flashlight, seeing nothing. The next morning, less than 50 yards from our camp, we found not only tiger tracks, but also the path of an elephant that had moved through a nearby bamboo thicket. We slept and hiked within a green curtain which effectively concealed the jungle's vast, secret life. I take that weekend as an emblem of my limited understanding; yet images and poems continue to weather out of my memory. I suppose they are my subconscious effort to say "what it was like," to corner experience and make it say its name.

I. A Jah Hut* Orders the Universe by Color

When he descended from Ala'ta'ala, the greatest God, Proman prayed to him. He asked God to create the world inside the ocean, the dome of the sky and the air that is blue. When he had prayed to God, God said to him, "It can be done, but you must gather the foam of the sea. When the foam of the sea is gathered, you must knead it until it is tightly packed. Knead it with the palm of your hand. Make the rock. Make the world."

—Jah Hut* creation myth, from *Tales of a Shaman*

Huil! All huil!
We crave permission to enter on this domain
and tie our nooses to these trees.

(traditional Malay deer hunting prayer)

*Jah Hut—aboriginal tribe in Peninsular Malaysia

A JAH HUT ORDERS THE UNIVERSE BY COLOR

Green are the islands of men
but red is the sea
of the world.
Black lies under red
and under the world.
Black is cow, fish, and snake.
Purple the moon.
Purple the sun.
Yellow the hole
in the foot of the sky
where sun and moon
pass through.
Below black and red
is the rock of the world.
It is no color.

IN MALAY FORESTS

Fear of snakes
sends us highstepping
up the trail.
Overhead
a Tualong tree
outstrips its rivals
for air and light
despite the strangler fig
growing from a crotch
at 200 feet.

All around
a silent life
rises and falls
beneath the airy bodies
of leaves.
Lianas, rattans, and creepers
send dense signals
where the slower self
still reads the book
of bramble and briar
and heartwood's sap
rises in tides
where no moon shows
nor any hand
leaflike goes.

ON ENTERING THE CENTRAL HIGHLANDS

Trees
a monotony of trees
where unnamed animals
marked by light and dark
wait patiently
to lift the spell
from men.

ORANG ASLI*

Above Tanah Rata's little stones
the highlands rise
and breathe the great forest
and its great trees.

Beneath those trees
I saw three boys
hunting birds with blowpipes,
wearing sneakers and jeans.

Orang asli
first men
caught in history's wash
beyond the broad banana leaves.

Surprise!
I stopped and stared.
They disappeared
in the mountain's aching air.

* Orang Asli—original men, indigenous people's name for themselves

ELLIPSIS

I don't know what
it was.
I waited
for it to rise
beyond the lianas
and sand flies.

Something bulged
the jungle's curtain.
I sat until
it overcame me,
like water hyacinths
the Buriganga.

CONVERSATION WITH THE SHAMAN

In the trees
away from the light
in the deep deep trees
inside the night
were your dreams good?
What did you dream
last night?

My soul leaped
with dreams
last night.
The man
with a sharp head
turned and leered
in the light.

Were your dreams good?
What did you dream
last night?

My soul roared with dreams
last night.
I looked the man
with a long tongue
in the face.
My body is sick
from the sight.

Were your dreams good?
What did you dream
last night?

My soul shook
with dreams
last night.

I saw the world
without its skin.
My body filled
with the height.

Were your dreams good?
What did you dream
last night?

My soul didn't
roam in dreams
last night.
It lay heavy
and thick
in the body's hut
last night.

Were your dreams good?
What did you dream
last night?

IN THE FINE BLUE WEATHER

two sea eagles
bare to the knee
took fish from the water
and tore them at their leisure
in a mangrove by the sea.

*BURUNG HAJI**

Unseen singer
lost in light,
your voice's frangipani
thin like invisibility
in the scented air.

The pilgrimage—
already miles within
you sing.

* Burung Haji—Pilgrimage Bird, a species of finch.

THE WORLD'S LARGEST FLOWER IS A PARASITE

Sabah Tower
tallest building on Borneo
rises from the deaths
of a billion trees,
flowers in the banks
of Tokyo and Manhattan.
Feeding on land and water
the tower grows.
Power beads like nectar
along its stem,
Weyerhaeuser, Foundation,
drip, drip
on the forest floor.
It sighs with vegetable sound
as the great trees
come down.
Merbau, Meranti, Balau
bine, bowl, and bower.

In the foothills of Kinabalu,
Rafflesia* keeps a secret life
vine within vine
waiting to effloresce
from dark buds
and fragile soil.
All the while
the silent tendrils take.
The vine's blood
becomes its own,
their two hearts beating
each to each,

the monstrous flower,
too late,
the only sign.

* The parasitic Rafflesia ("corpse flower") is the world's largest flower.

A DREAM OF TIGERS

The mounds begin
to move,
not earth at all.
I look for trees
to climb.
Nothing but
low-slung frangipani
and padi grass.

They move like
dream tigers,
incredible rushes
and numbing charges.
I can only stand
while they brush by.

Somehow I am safe.
I slip into a stagnant pool,
water a green roof
above my head.
Tigers bounce off
like harmless hail.

JUNGLE LETTER TO MY WIFE

(For Jeannie, 1944–2010)

There was something
I had wanted to say,
after all the body's
noise and fall,
but the screen
inside our years
was too deep to see,
and now too late
to tear away.

The lives we lived
and those we dreamed
soared together,
a strangler fig
two hundred feet
above the jungle floor
whose slow aerial
life brings down
the greatest tree.

In the noise and joy
of all our hours
the terrible secret
hummed unheard
within you, a seed
some wayward bird
dropped carelessly
in the warm bark high
up your body's tree.

II. Pulau Pinang

George Town [is a] living testimony to the multi-cultural heritage and tradition of Asia, and European colonial influences. This multi-cultural tangible and intangible heritage is expressed in the great variety of religious buildings of different faiths, ethnic quarters, the many languages, worship and religious festivals, dances, costumes, art and music, food, and daily life.

Criterion iii of UNESCO's designation of George Town, Penang, Malaysia as a World Heritage City.

Pulau Pinang Terus Maju

(continuous progress for Penang Island), slogan of the local government.

THE PRESENCE OF SNOW IN THE TROPICS

We awoke this morning
cold
finding heavy snow
bending the naïve branches
of starfruit and ciku.
Torpid geckos
chirruped like night birds
in dismay.
Neighbors
in sandals
had frostbitten toes.

But it was going fast.
Already the earth's middle
bulged toward the sun,
satiated with its
nocturnal binge
of cold and ice.
The intermittent drops
upon the tile grew quicker
until, like rain,
they swept through storm drains,
themselves their own monsoon.

The earth relaxed.
It was perpetual July again.
We alone,
poised with sled and boots,
felt the loss
of seasons
in our bodies'
deep stone.

PULAU PINANG TERUS MAJU

The rhythm here
is pile driver.
The molar-jarring
ring of steel on steel
to the percussion
of steam
follows me
from the pilings
of the new bridge
at Bayan Lepas
to Jalan Sultan Ahmad Shah.

They are never still.
Days tick by to their beat.
Traffic lunges forward
with the same brutality.
Earth and coral-headed rock
give way slowly.
The island winces
under the blows,
lurches sharply
with the weight
of highrise.

Hemmed by mountains
and sea
the rich go mad.
They pound huge pillars
into rock and
blast the tops
of hills,
blowing forests
into the sea.

Displaced monkeys
line the roads.

Malaysia needs capital,
the P.M. says.
Bang. Bang.
Let the West
feed the monkeys.
Bang. Bang.
Land, timber, money.
Bang. Bang. Bang.
The steam-driven litany goes.

And also go
tigers, elephants
and great upland trees.
Cengal, Sereya,
Merbau, Meranti,
bringing down
in their tree deaths
the lesser larak and tersina
felled to lie in ruin.

In a shop on Chulia Street
hang the dried penis
and testicles of an ape.
Mercedes queue up
for potency after dark.
No one believes anymore,
but always
the first law
puts the hand
before the life.

NAVARATHRI*

Today
the noodle woman
and her sister
were subtracted
from the human sum,
their Honda 90
sent spinning
across slick pavement
like a stricken dog,
their limbs adjusted
permanently askew.

The bas kilang*
had its own trajectory,
the motorcycle less
than vulnerable.
The driver may have regretted,
but the fine disharmony
of thoughtless action
is worked out
in heat and motion.

Billowing black smoke
dwarfing all else
on the narrow streets,
the buses are not to be taken lightly.
And so,
two cautious women are dead
while young boys
on jazzed-up Suzukis
slalom through
tightly moving traffic
in their own kamakaze
versions of thrill.

Khakti,
why not them?
But the inertia
of the great dieseled body
simply cut down
what was in its way.
The slowest
the easiest
scattered
upon the water
like chum
for rising sharks.

One thousand three hundred
and eighty-four years ago
Muhammad journeyed
from Mecca to Medina
and the year began,
but Pearl Hill
is silent in its mists.
The island
sways on its stem.
Rain washes the streets
each night
and tells us that
there is no struggle.

* Navarathri—Tamil Hindu holy day sacred to Khakti (Kali), celebrating the triumph of good
  over evil.
* Bas kilang—diesel bus

SAMSUI WOMEN*

Beside the road
to Ayer Itam
two Chinese women labor
in a ditch of dirt and stone.
On the median
two Malay men
operate a mower and a broom.
The morning sun
rebuilds its room
then enters
and re-enters.

The brutal asymmetry of color
works through the body
like a worm
no purgative can dislodge.
Yet the sisterhood of labor
will not fade.
We see them gloved,
heads and arms covered
against the sun
working beyond the priesthood of men
in some nunnery of the mind.

The future falls
dulls itself
in the rubble of ditches.
Science flows past in flood.
The two women stop
to cover noses and mouths
against the dust rising
from six pound hoes.
History does not move.

Their mattocks might
as well be stone.

Now they hit upon a rock.
Two hours later
there is another.
The sun burns
through the equatorial lens
as though it
never sets.
Another hour
and the great rock
arches out of the dirt
like a buried elephant.

Finally it is quitting time.
Earth and rock
hum in the sun
waiting for night
and the cooling shade,
recharge their inertia
for the coming day.
The women are
devoured by dieseled
buses too knotted
ever to be undone.

* Samsui women immigrated to the Malaysian peninsula from China in the early 20th century
  seeking work and independence. They did much of the hard labor establishing Malaya and
  Singapore.

DOWNTOWN MANILA AFTER
BENIGNO AQUINO'S ASSASSINATION*

August 21, 1983

The traffic writes its
own eulogy
in heat, tangle, and noise
despite the pause
to let the blood flow out.

And homeward
the brave jeepneys
forge their way
flags waving,
flashing their silver palominos.

* Aquino was the opposition leader against the regime of Ferdinand Marcos. His murder led
  to a revolution and the restoration of democracy in the Philippines.

THE NEWNESS OF HER SURPRISE
(Míng chún shíh wáng)*

She is now míng chún,
a favored one
fallen through the net
of family and money.
Slowly she spends her
capital of culture.
The glamor of the past
buoys her
in the current,
Chiang Kai-shek
at her father's table
and winters in Canton.
Gay cloth
upon the stream.

The scramble
for morning noodles
and the evening mee
is divided
one million times.
So we see her
sinking
in the crowded streets,
a face
in the torrent
of faces,
visible only
by the newness
of her surprise.

* Míng chún shíh wáng—loosely, from the Hokkien: to exist in name only.

POLO IN THE TANG

Mu Tsung*
frightened by a eunuch's
death beneath the hooves
never walked again.

How could a eunuch
bring down the Tang?
But the emperor
saw a great snake
gorged on eggs.
The glazed stare
caught him in the saddle,
stopped the side-stroke,
the red ball
rebounding from the wood,
the curving moonstick in its arc.
He was alone
on a plaza like a mirror
or a whetstone.
The snake
whose name he forgot
remembered the king,
the drums and gongs silent,
the banners of east and west
drooping in the windless air.

It was the cucumber
snake smell
that dropped him,
and the gaze
empty as the court.
He felt fear
enter his horse
through its hard hooves,

saw its eyes roll whitely.
The paving stones
bounced him
crisper than the ball.
The crowd swelled and broke
but saw eunuch
not snake.

The snake
slow eater
began a long meal.
The emperor in his bed
lingered for yet another year.

* My version of one of the legends about the death of Tang emperor Muzong in 824.

PULAU PINANG* ADRIFT

Each evening
clouds from the hills
bring down the rain.
We move to cover
and sit to see
them in.
The sea heaves itself up
on the shore
slowly aroused by rain.

Fresh and salt
the waters blend,
the flood's great curve
traced down mountainsides
in gullies
deep as sores.
Water seeks water
with all the grief
of land and sea.

Water
has cut her free
of the earth's belly.
Pulau Pinang
floats as easily
upon the sea
as day on night,
her earth-stem a keel,
her mountains sails.

* Pulau Pinang—Pinang Island

EVENING ON THE KLONG PAKANONG*

Herded by heat
houses line up
along the canal
like trees seeking water
beneath the water's bed.

From the temple steps
saffroned monks
stroke the backs
of great catfish
fattened on daily loaves.
They reach out
and the water boils.
Downstream
giant nets levered up empty
go spangled in the light.
Naked children
bask like turtles
in the wooden boats.
Families pause
in the peace of water.

Wildness retreats
to the streets
of Bangkok,
waits like a tiger
beneath the skin.

* Klong Pakanong—A canal near Bangkok.

POEMS

*(Batu Ferringhi)**

I've read that all
the tools ever used
in the world
are still being made,
a wheel for a chariot
a flint knife
a bone hook.

It is comforting
to believe that
what we make
persists, stubbornly
beyond the
hard parenthesis
of our lives.

On the Portuguese Rocks
far below
a man casts a net.
Each time it makes
a silver circle
10,000 years old
on the sea.

* Batu Ferringhi—Portuguese Rocks, Penang.

EDAITHI*

Where rubber and rambutan
once flourished
she keeps her own paths
through Tanjong Bungah.*
The only grass now borders
asphalt and concrete,
but still the cycle goes.
The habit of 3,000 years
ignores houses
sprouting like fungi,
the traffic hurtling into
confusion along the coast.

The cattle do not hurry.
She prods them
only when the grass
is gone.
Still my daughters wait.
They like the gentleness
of cattle
raised in towns.
There is the sway
of brown haunches,
the velvet skin,
and the girls

who offer leftovers
in plates
to great soft lips
and tongues.
The cattle are polite
but the old Tamil woman
eyes us.
Beef eaters!

She knows the calm
of cattle
living with women
beyond the knives of men.

Around the bovine flesh
my daughters celebrate
the lifting of the curse
which once could bind them
skin and hair
to the hides of cows.
The soft flanks
give way
before the girls'
excited dance.
The wand is raised.
The cows pass on.

* Edaithi—from the Tamil, loosely, a female cowherd.
* Tanjong Bungah—neighborhood in George Town.

GANAPATHY*

The way to the sea
is littered
with boulders
like browsing elephants
on the hillside,
gray skin
rough as sandpaper,
or shark.
Once, twice
my daughters
brush stone
raising blood.
Sandflies hum
about the wounds
more malevolent than mosquitoes.

More rocks
and the sun
heats the path
like an oven,
we its
poor white loaves.
Each of us begins
to fade
in the tug and trip
of sand.
But one great stone
turns its grinning head—
Vinayaga Chathurthi! *
The way to the sea
lies free.

* Vinayaga Chathurthi—Holy day for the worship of elephant-headed Ganapathy (Ganesh)
  who removes obstacles for believers.

ANG POW*

It is the twenty-fourth day
of the twelfth moon
and the Kitchen God
has begun his annual
visit to heaven.
But Xiao Lin
is our kitchen god
serving up the
special steamboat
to welcome in the year.
We dip tiny
eggs of quail,
slivers of freshly-killed chicken,
huge prawns hauled squirming
from the sea last night,
baby onions and little
haystacks of bean sprouts
into the boiling broth.

Later, she says,
there will be ang pows
for the children.
No, no, we protest,
you are our ang pow!
You and this marvelous pot
puffing in the table's center
like a small engine of love.

* Ang Pow—A gift of money in a red envelope.

PENANG, 30 YEARS LATER

Our old house in Penang
is now abandoned
wearing down under
the soft lick
of sun and water,
its cool tile floors
defaced by the mindless
graffiti of rats,
mold's smudged
black fingerprints
on all the walls and doors.

Alive again, you
stand on the balcony
in the modest shorts
and polo shirt that
scandalized the neighbors
a quarter century ago.
You watch as I
wash our old Cortina
and spray our daughters
who circle giggling
in their batik bikinis.

We are full
of our lives
in the exotic.
We see only
the left side
of our parenthesis.

III. The Stone

Since the objects of sense are merely emanations of Brahman, to know them in themselves is not enough. Since all the actions of men are but phases of the universal process of creation, action alone is not enough.

—The *Mundaka Upanishad*

THE STONE

When you were born a tall handsome woman with the slenderest of fingers gave you back your stone. She placed it on your tongue like an aspirin and held your mouth shut and stroked your throat until you had to swallow. The stone is smooth, shaped and pressed by the weight of all the world's waters, rolled by the journeys of all the world's rivers to the sea. Inside you it becomes a perfect sphere the size of a pea. A thin layer of cells coats it so that you can carry it all your life like a shark carries souvenirs from all its meals.

When you are ready to die the woman will come again. She will still be handsome and her fingers will still be sharp. With incredible ease, and drawing very little blood, she will reach through your side and pluck out the stone, now big as a cherry. It has absorbed all your days and nights which give it the color of pale blood. It is your stone, but she will keep it for you. When she swallows the stone your heart will burst. When you are ready to try again, she will come to you. She will put the stone on your tongue and hold your mouth and stroke and stroke your throat. It will be harder to swallow. You will always wish for a smaller stone.

SAMADHI*

Find the deep pool,
the one where the
river has eaten
a meal of limestone
and left behind the
bones of a bluff
lying calmly in the water
like languorous buffalo.

Become a glowing red carp
living in a deep still pool.
Hang suspended in the place
where it is neither dark nor light.
Then move faster
than the dragonfly
that kisses the face
of the pool at noon.

When you find that pool
and become that carp,
move neither against the stream
where the rapids rattle their stones,
nor go with it where the current dies
and the banks flatten
and the water's mouth
is filled with mud.

Make no bargains.
Make no trades.
The pool is a stone
tossed to earth
from a great height.

You are the jewel
that glistens
when the geode cracks.

* Samadhi—a state of deep meditation, enlightenment

IN THE SNAKE TEMPLE

> ... and there you will find snakes coiling
> around the altar ... as if intoxicated by the
> smell of burning incense.
>
> —*Penang for the Visitor*

Until the joss stick moved
I had thought snake temple
was metaphor,
like the temple of God.
But before me
a Wagler's viper
translated itself
from stone to flesh.
Monks moved carelessly
among the miracles,
still figures of speech
to their bare heels,
while all about
the hieroglyphs
of stone scripture
undid themselves.

Then I heard the secret
epiphanies of snakes
whispered in the room,
and like my brothers
those exegetes of *Mark*
in the hills
of East Tennessee,
was wracked
by the rhythm
of tongues.

CREATION STORY

To clear a spot in chaos
for creation, Vishnu
ladled all the demons
out of the churning sea
of milk that would
become the universe,
but not before
they fouled it.
So he created fish
to eat their excrement
and clean the sea.
For a while the milk
was good again,
but then he made people
who invented nets and
caught all the fish
and fried them up.
Undigested, the demon's feces
got into their cells
and drove them mad
so that they began
to beat and tear
each other.
Vishnu put his head
in all four hands.
He'd have to think
of something else.

ON THE PEARL RIVER PROMENADE

Zhuhai, China

> All is a procession,
> the universe is a procession
> with measured and perfect motion.
>
> —*I Sing the Body Electric*, Walt Whitman

The Pearl river is dissolving
in the South China Sea,
over the pearls of Guangzhou
under the pylons of Zhuhai
past the ships at Macau.
The machinery of the world
turns noisily,
but the Great Procession
is as silent
as the sea.

Molecules of the balustrade
secretly ignite
the fuses of the palms.
Stones of the promenade
slowly wear away.
Strolling couples
divide and re-divide
as they digitize
their lives beside
the mindless sea.

Large bony fish
with sharp bronze scales
and fins like saws
cruise just below
the dingy surface

and look up.
White sea birds floating
like urgent flotsam
watch without blinking
empty fishlike eyes.

In the persistent haze
a ship on the horizon's line
sails at 20 knots
due east into the sky,
its passengers wild
with voiceless surprise.

THE PARENTHESIS

Before we were born
our parenthesis
was already made,
cut into an endless sheet
of old boilerplate
that lies in the shade
of a mile-high tree.
It has killed all
the grass beneath it.
The face of the metal
is pitted like the moon.
Clouds of rust
roam across
its airless space.

The marks are deep
in the steel
and have shown
like silver forever.
While we are here
we can see clearly
the left side.
Each morning we wake
believing we live
in infinite time
even though
the right side
gleams unseen
only minutes away.

THAIPUSAM*

I.

Subramania's House*

Lord Subramania's house
has many rooms.
Its air thickens
with incense and drums.
Gay kavadis float
like flowers
on the crowd's
bright stream.
Sivite eyes glaze
with exhaustion.
Slowly penitent flesh
gives up its burden.

Above,
the bell
of Waterfall Temple
beats as loud
as the blood
of women
gathered with Nikons
around the altar
of ash.
The piercing
of male flesh
has some appeal.

Somewhere in the crowd
one Tamil woman
cannot wait.
She screams and
energy rises like heat

from the street.
A man faints
at the altar
a five foot spear
rattling in his teeth.
Ashes float in the air.

    II.

Rama Nama Satya Hai*

He squats calmly,
Siva, Vishnu and Brahma
heavy on his flesh.
Silent now
he begins his vow
as the crowd
flows by in festival.
His mouth hums
with the taste of steel
and what his body knows.
The drums are water
which lifts and carries him.

Nearby vendors hawk
pictures of Siva, Jesus
and Brooke Shields.
The kavadi
burns like a flame
upon his shoulders.
The five kilometers to
Waterfall Temple red-shift
beyond the heat and noise.
Inside his head

is a small room where
he must stand and wait.

Pain,
a beautiful woman,
speaks crimson words
he must not hear.
The temple steps elongate.
The crowd chants
the names of God
and the bell answers
with hard metal words.
Ashes settle alike
on the curious
and the faithful.

* Thaipusam—Tamil Hindu festival known for its extreme mortification of the flesh.
* Subramania—a Hindu god.
* Rama Nama Satya Hai—the name of God is Truth

WESAK DAY*

The bus opens itself
and we flow into
Kek Lok Si
the Temple of Supreme Bliss,
surging, shoving
toward immortality.
The Pagoda of 10,000 Buddhas
stands over Ayer Itam*
like a wedding cake
shining in the tropic sun.
Tourists jockey with cameras.
Believers with joss sticks
add to the haze of
of incense and heat that
refracts us from ourselves.
Expectation ripples
like electricity
through the crowd.
But I do not notice
the intense longing.
I do not see
the Goddess of Mercy
rising like a calm white
mountain above us.

* Wesak Day—Buddha's birthday
* Ayer Itam—a neighborhood of George Town, Penang.

MAYA

The cattle stand facing east.
Their bodies shine like lumps
of coal in the rising sun.
They stand in the center of the worn

geometry of their path. Sun
warms their backs, making
light upon them tremble.
Hard hooves have vanished.

Around them the yellow heads
of dandelions collapse and rid
themselves of ragged bodies
rising from milky roots.

Nearby the tight brown coats
of cattails emphatic on the margins
of the pond have begun to dissolve
into flakes of air-borne down.

I am here watching, wearing
my heaviness like a coat.
Hard matter in its home around
me seems poised to disappear.

FESTIVAL OF THE HUNGRY GHOSTS*

In the seventh moon
Mu Lien pierced
the thin space
dividing the worlds
and plucked out
his mother, a prisoner
of starving demons.

But brave Mu Lien
ruptured an invisible membrane
as he passed through,
releasing hungry spirits
into this world
to wander furiously
searching for food.

We burn Phor Thor Kong
the Demon King
in the streets each night,
but each day he is back
among us, gorging himself
on the cloying sweetmeats
we hide deep inside.

* Festival of the Hungry Ghosts—Chinese festival celebrating the release of the spirits of the
dead to feast upon offerings of food.

SUMMER SOLSTICE

(for Yu Huan)

Minute-by-minute
my days will
now grow shorter,
while you,
following the sun's track,
will mile-by-mile
give back
the day we had together.
On the darkest day
of the year
I will walk out
and look 7000
miles west
across the frozen space
of winter's weather
and taste again
the hidden sweetness
of your black bean cakes.

THE SNAKE TEMPLE REVISITED

It is the birthday of Chor Soo Kong.
In the sanctuary
he touches the blue skin
of his belly
and smiles
to see the faithful
gather in the rain
outside his door.
All day they come and go
filling his bowl
with joss sticks and fruit.
In every room
incense is a cloud
whose warning
burns the eyes
and hides the temple doors.
Now smoke gathers
the will of God.
Forms of the dead
drawn by fruit
and prayers
glow like lanterns
in the fog.
Snakes lie stupefied
by divinity
in the altar trees.
Worshippers emerge
tearful in the air
while Jerry Lee Lewis
bangs out *Great Balls O' Fire*
from the juice stand
just below.

KRISHNA CONTEMPLATES THE
UNION CARBIDE DISASTER AT BHOPAL

December 2, 1984

I had not thought it,
therefore
did not believe it.
And died
a whole forest of people,
in what war?

Not for a moment
can a man stand still.
This is the world.
Be a warrior, kill desire!
But whoever draws the bow
must know the arrow.

WORDS AS CLEAN AS FISH

I sat in a blue boat
upon dark water.
To the fish
I was a cloud
or hand
drifting over their firmament.

Carp lay under ledges.
Turtles burrowed in mud.
Mussels breathed long trails
of carbon dioxide.
Whole cities of moss
waved solemnly to me.

I could not see
but felt them there,
and began
to say them,
each in its heaven,
each as it is—

Carp

Turtle

Mussel

Moss

The words floated.
They made
perfect spheres
that rose in the air
like the mussels'
breathings.

I pulled up my anchor,
began the long pull
to shore.
Words
as clean as fish
darted away.

CHIAM SEE*

Remember the properties of water.
Your present state
is like a fish slowly
becoming a dragon.
Scales grow and thicken,
the body draws itself out,
ventral fins become legs.
The surface of things
is as smooth as glass,
but below
the current wraps cedars
thicker than a man
around the river's
granite bones.
Someone or something
lost long ago
rises toward you.

To find luck
go south or east.
Go as a boat goes,
go where the wind blows.

* Chaim See—literally, a "fortunate forecast," sold in the Thai Buddhist Wat in Penang.

YALA, TSUNAMI*

Near the beach
where the wave
embraced fishermen
in their huts
and plucked tourists
from the sand,
a leopard slept
away the heat
on the limb
of a Banian tree,
dogs lay in the road
stupefied by worms,
and I dreamed
of the room
where you died
in Kentucky.
In the darkness
your bed
floated out to sea.
All day
abhaya Buddhas
having passed
through Enlightenment
had raised their
stone hands—
All is well.

On the far side
of the trees
the sea slowly stirred
its turgid soup of the lost.

* Yala National Park in Sri Lanka. The tsunami is the horrific one of December 26, 2004.

WATCHING THE PROCESSION OF THE SILVER CHARIOT*

Where will I stand
to see
when I die?
The stone pillar
with its green leprosy
of mold
where we sat
to watch
the Silver Chariot
come by?

And saw the
women in their saris
siting on the curb,
yellow, green, and blue.
Where will I stand
to see
as the crowds
swell by?

How will I
fix my eyes
when I die?
I see the odors
of spice and incense
where they rise.
I smell the greens,
the reds, the indigos,
then...

let go.

* The Silver Chariot is a large silver altar paraded through the streets to begin the festival of
   Thaipusam.

ACKNOWLEDGMENTS

The author is grateful to the publications in which the following poems initially appeared:

Chelsea: "Polo in theTang," "Edaithi"

Cincinnati Poetry Review: "The World's Largest Flower is a Parasite"

The Journal of Kentucky Studies: "Pulau Pinang Adrift"

Kentucky Philological Review: "Words as Clean as Fish," "The Presence of Snow in the Tropics"

Rhino: "In the Snake Temple"

Rilke's Children: "The Presence of Snow in the Tropics," "In Malay Forests," "Orang Asli," "Chiam See," reprinted in *The Presence of Snow in the Tropics*

Newsletter of the Singapore Buddhist Association: "The Stone," reprinted in *Rilke's Children* and *The Presence of Snow in the Tropics*

Stand Magazine: "Navarathri," "Samsui Women" (as "A Sisterhood of Labor"), reprinted in *The Presence of Snow in the Tropics*

The Kentucky Anthology: "In Malay Forests," reprinted from *The Presence of Snow in the Tropics*

ABOUT THE AUTHOR

Joe Survant is Professor Emeritus at Western Kentucky University. He is the author of seven collections of poems, most recently, *View from the Stork Building*, from Larkspur Press. He is the winner of the Miller Williams Poetry Prize from the University of Arkansas Press and a recipient of grants from the Kentucky Arts Council, The Asia Foundation, the Fulbright Foundation, and the NEH. Individual poems have been published in Malaysia, China, Japan, Singapore and the U.K., as well as in the U.S. He served as Kentucky's Poet Laureate 2002–2004.

www.ingramcontent.com/pod-product-compliance
Lightning Source LLC
Chambersburg PA
CBHW020334130626
46549CB00003B/1175